LAKE CLASSICS

*Great American
Short Stories II*

WITHDRAWN

Herman
MELVILLE

Stories retold by Prescott Hill
Illustrated by James Balkovek

LAKE EDUCATION
Belmont, California

LAKE CLASSICS

Great American Short Stories I

Washington Irving, Nathaniel Hawthorne, Mark Twain, Bret Harte, Edgar Allan Poe, Kate Chopin, Willa Cather, Sarah Orne Jewett, Sherwood Anderson, Charles W. Chesnutt

Great American Short Stories II

Herman Melville, Stephen Crane, Ambrose Bierce, Jack London, Edith Wharton, Charlotte Perkins Gilman, Frank R. Stockton, Hamlin Garland, O. Henry, Richard Harding Davis

Great British and Irish Short Stories

Arthur Conan Doyle, Saki (H. H. Munro), Rudyard Kipling, Katherine Mansfield, Thomas Hardy, E. M. Forster, Robert Louis Stevenson, H. G. Wells, John Galsworthy, James Joyce

Great Short Stories from Around the World

Guy de Maupassant, Anton Chekhov, Leo Tolstoy, Selma Lagerlöf, Alphonse Daudet, Mori Ogwai, Leopoldo Alas, Rabindranath Tagore, Fyodor Dostoevsky, Honoré de Balzac

Cover and Text Designer: Diann Abbott

Library of Congress Catalog Number: 94-075022
ISBN 1-56103-014-7
Printed in the United States of America
1 9 8 7 6 5 4 3 2 1

CONTENTS

❦ Lake Classic Short Stories ❧

"The universe is made of stories, not atoms."
> —Muriel Rukeyser

"The story's about you."
> —Horace

Everyone loves a good story. It is hard to think of a friendlier introduction to classic literature. For one thing, short stories are *short*—quick to get into and easy to finish. Of all the literary forms, the short story is the least intimidating and the most approachable.

Great literature is an important part of our human heritage. In the belief that this heritage belongs to everyone, *Lake Classic Short Stories* are adapted for today's readers. Lengthy sentences and paragraphs are shortened. Archaic words are replaced. Modern punctuation and spellings are used. Many of the longer stories are abridged. In all the stories, painstaking care has been taken to preserve the author's unique voice.

Lake Classic Short Stories have something for everyone. The hundreds of stories in the collection cover a broad terrain of themes, story types, and styles. Literary merit was a deciding factor in story selection. But no story was included unless it was as enjoyable as it was instructive. And special priority was given to stories that shine light on the human condition.

Each book in the *Lake Classic Short Stories* is devoted to the work of a single author. Little-known stories of merit are included with famous old favorites. Taken as a whole, the collected authors and stories make up a rich and diverse sampler of the story-teller's art.

Lake Classic Short Stories guarantee a great reading experience. Readers who look for common interests, concerns, and experiences are sure to find them. Readers who bring their own gifts of perception and appreciation to the stories will be doubly rewarded.

❧ Herman Melville ❧
(1819–1891)

About the Author

Herman Melville was born in New York City, the third of eight children. His father's death in 1832 ended the boy's hopes of a college education.

To help support the family, he went to sea at the age of 19. "A whale ship was my Yale College and my Harvard," he said many years later. After 18 months, he deserted the whaling ship. Luckily he was taken in by a tribe of natives in the Marquesas Islands. He spent six weeks with them, and he later based his exciting novel *Typee* on this experience.

Melville also spent some time in Tahiti and Hawaii before returning home. Many of his books (*Omoo, Mardi, Pierre, Moby Dick, Redburn, White-Jacket,* and *Billy Budd*) were at least partly based on these early experiences.

Melville was very popular in the early part of his career. As he got older, however, the substance of his novels got more complicated. Instead of exciting adventure stories, he began to turn out tales that were heavy with symbolism. By the time he died in 1891, he had lost his popularity and was largely unappreciated.

About 30 years after his death, however, Melville was suddenly "discovered" again. His novel *Moby Dick,* the story of Captain Ahab's quest for the white whale, is now considered one of America's greatest books. The opening line, "Call me Ishmael," is one of the most famous lines in literature.

If you like strong characters who fight against even stronger forces, you'll enjoy Melville's stories. His characters might not always win, but they'll fight to the end.

The Piazza

What is reality and what is
illusion? Sometimes it's not
easy to tell the difference.
In this story, a lonely man
lets his imagination get the
best of his common sense.
Will he find the "magic
land" that he thinks he sees
in the distance? Or will he
find a very different kind of
place?

"As I looked out from the piazza, I saw a ring of light on the distant mountain."

The Piazza

When I moved to the country, I went to live in a farmhouse. It was a fine old place, except for one thing. It needed a piazza—a big covered porch. I have always liked piazzas. I feel they combine the coziness of indoors with the freedom of outdoors.

Mostly I missed having a piazza because the countryside around my house was so beautiful. In fact, artists often came from miles around to paint pictures of it. A piazza would have offered me the best view of the scenery.

11

The house was more than 70 years old when I moved into it. It was built in the middle of the woods. Since then, all the trees around it have been cleared away, except for one old elm. Whoever built the house placed it in just the right spot—even if he didn't know it then. With the trees gone, there are four wonderful views from the house. If the house had been built even 100 feet from where it stands, those views would have been wasted.

To the east were distant hillsides covered with trees. They were dark and dull in winter, but green in spring and summer. They blazed with color in the fall of the year.

To the south stretched an apple orchard. In the month of May it was white with apple blossoms. In the month of October, it was a deep green with flashes of red dotting it.

To the west I looked out across a sloping pasture. It was gray and bare in the winter, but streaks of green appeared there in springtime. As summer ended and fall began, the pasture became golden.

But the best view of all was to the north. Looking in that direction, I could see a half-circle of mountains. One mountain stood out above the others. To me it looked like Charlemagne, the mighty king of old Europe. The smaller mountains surrounding it seemed like his knights.

Charlemagne was a kingly mountain indeed. On clear days I could watch him being crowned with gold at both sunrise and sunset.

To enjoy my views, I knew that a piazza was needed. Does not an art gallery need benches so people can rest as they enjoy the paintings? Beauty is not something to be enjoyed in a hurry. If my house had a piazza, I would have a place to put an easy chair. There I could take time to enjoy the view.

During my first year in the house, I often sat on a hillside to look at the mountains. There were wild strawberries and blue violets there. I even planted some honeysuckle. But it was a damp, shadowy place. The view was fine, but I caught a cold from sitting there.

A piazza must be had.

The house was big, but my wallet was small. I could not afford to build a piazza around the whole house. But all was not lost. If I could not enjoy *four* views to the fullest, at least I could fully enjoy *one*. I had enough money to build a piazza along one side of the house.

But which side should it be?

That was easy to decide. I chose the north side with the view of Charlemagne.

In the month of March, the carpenters set to work at building my piazza. I remember how their noses turned blue from the cold. And I remember how they laughed at me for wanting my piazza

built on the north side of the house.
When my neighbors saw what was
happening, they laughed too. "Building
a piazza on the *north*?" one neighbor
said. "A winter piazza! You'll want to
make sure you wear warm mittens
out there. That's the coldest side of
the house."

He was right, of course. But what
better place to sit and keep cool on a hot
summer afternoon?

In the winter, the north was also the
windiest side. The cold wind howled in
from that direction and blew the snow
about like the finest flour. But that was
all right with me. The weather reminded
me of my days as a sailor, sailing around
Cape Horn. I walked the piazza then as
I used to walk the deck in a winter storm.

In the summer, I was also reminded of
my days aboard ship. As I looked from
my piazza, I saw a sea of grass below the
mountains. The blue shadows of the

mountains looked like the blue waves at
sea. At noon, there was rarely any wind.
It was like being on a calm ocean. In the
afternoon a breeze often came up. Then
the fuzzy dandelions looked like puffs of
ocean spray.

Sometimes, during one of these
afternoons, I would notice a strange
house in the distance. Many such small
places were half-hidden in the woods.
Catching sight of one was like catching
sight of the sail of a strange ship at sea.

And that reminds me of the autumn I
went to see such a house. It turned out
to be a voyage to fairyland. Even though
it was a true voyage, it may seem as
though I made it up.

From the piazza, it was not always
easy to know just what I was seeing in
the distance. Sometimes I would think
that an object—a house, perhaps—was
on a hillside. Then later in the day the

light would be different. Now the house might seem to be on a mountain top.

Sometimes a mountain might stand out by itself. At other times it might seem to be only the slope of a larger mountain. When the light changed or the weather changed, the view seemed to change as well. Those mountains seemed to play hide-and-seek right before my eyes.

The strange house I saw that autumn day also played hide-and-seek. I had been living in my farmhouse for a year before I noticed it. The air was not clear that day. Smoke from a distant forest fire had drifted across the hillsides. It was late in the season. The bright orange, red, and yellow colors of the autumn leaves were already beginning to fade.

As I looked out from the piazza, I saw a ring of light on the distant mountain. Everything around that bright spot was in shade. I thought it must be haunted: a magic place where fairies dance.

I did not catch sight of the house again until the following spring. It was in the month of May. There had been rain showers on the mountain all morning, and now there was a rainbow. I noticed that one end of the rainbow was just at the spot where I had seen the ring of light. Well, I thought, that must be a lucky place. I knew the old story about the pot of gold at the end of the rainbow.

I pointed out the house to a neighbor. "It seems like a magic place to me," I said.

He said it looked like an old barn—one that was falling apart.

But I knew better. I had never been there, but I had my own ideas about it.

A few days after that, I looked out at the mountains at sunrise. I could see a ray of light coming from that magic spot. It looked like light shining on glass. I knew then that it was not a barn, as my neighbor had thought. And certainly it was not falling apart. It had to be a house. Maybe it was old and empty, but I was sure it was a house.

Not long after that I looked out again from my piazza. This time there was a stronger gleam of light in the same place. I thought I knew what it was. It had to be coming from a newly shingled roof.

And that must mean that the house was not empty. Someone was living there.

From time to time, I would try to find that gleaming spot again. Sometimes I would take a rest from my reading and search for it. But it never seemed to come into view, and I was sorry about that. That sight had always brought pleasant thoughts to my mind.

It was a long time before I had the chance to look for the magic spot. For some weeks I was sick in bed, and my room faced in a different direction.

At last, in September, I was well again. I went out to my piazza one morning to enjoy the view. The first thing I saw was a little flock of sheep walking across the hillside. Then I saw a neighbor's children following after them. I guessed they were going to pick nuts or berries. "How sweet a day!" I thought.

Then suddenly I saw again the golden flash of sunlight on glass. It was that magic spot—the land of fairies!

Well, I thought, the queen of the fairies must be there. Or maybe just some happy mountain girl lived in the house. At any rate, it would be a pleasant place to visit. After being sick for so long, a trip would do me good. Then and there I decided I would set out on a trip to fairyland—a trip to the rainbow's end.

I didn't know what road to take, but I knew the direction. And so I began my voyage of adventure. Instead of a boat, I had my horse. With the sun still low in the sky, we headed out on a road going north.

After a while the road ended, but that did not stop us. We followed trails made by cows and sheep. Then we came to a pasture and found our way blocked by an old log fence. The logs were green with moss. They looked liked something that had been fished up from a sunken wreck at sea. I moved them out of the way, and we continued on our travels.

For the moment, I had lost sight of the golden window, but I knew we were headed for it. Even in the woods, I could see the top of Charlemagne in the distance.

We followed a stream for a while, and then found another road. We passed an empty sawmill. It was old and falling apart. Vines grew all over it, almost hiding it from view.

After that road ended, we climbed up through an apple orchard. My horse stopped from time to time to eat apples from the ground. I tasted one myself and found it very sweet.

Finally we came to a place where the brush was very thick. Here, there was no path at all. I could get through the brush by crawling, but my horse could not. So I tied him to a tree and continued on by foot.

At first, I made my way by crawling under the brush and pushing through it. Then the going got even harder. I had to climb steep, rocky slopes. For a while I stopped to catch my breath. I needed the rest. It had been a long, hard walk, and still no fairyland in sight.

Then I continued on, following the path of some yellow birds. Finally I came to the top of a hill. By then I was feeling quite tired indeed, but suddenly my spirits lifted. I could see a zigzag path ahead of me. It was half covered over with blueberry bushes. Away off at the top of the path I could see a little gray cottage.

As I came nearer I saw that it was an old building with a sharply sloped roof. One of the slopes was covered with green moss. This slope was on the north side of the cottage.

The south slope was newly shingled. My guess had been right. Here was the shiny roof slope that I had seen from my piazza!

There were no doors or windows on the north side of the cottage. That north wall was as green with moss as the roof that sloped above it. The front door was on the south side of the house. The stone base of the house seemed to blend into the ground next to it. The cottage itself was unpainted wood. It was gray from age and the weather. It, too, seemed to blend into its surroundings.

There was no fence anywhere in sight. Green ferns were the only things nearby. Beyond them were the woods, and beyond the woods were the mountains. Beyond the mountains was nothing but sky, sky, sky. The house seemed to be part of nature. There was a pile of birch wood in front of it, piled up loosely to dry. Wild berry bushes grew among the silvery sticks of birch. The ferns almost filled the path to the house.

I was wearing the same white pants I wore in my sailing days. They didn't stay white for long. As I started up the path, I slipped and fell. The green ferns stained the knees of the pants.

The door to the house was open. As I looked in, I could see a girl sitting alone at the window next to the door. The window was very dusty and streaked. Cobwebs partly covered the upper panes. The girl was busy sewing. Her cheeks were very pale.

When I spoke, I took her by surprise. At first, she gave me a shy look and said nothing. But she invited me in by brushing off the stool next to her with her apron.

I nodded my thanks and entered. I sat down, but did not speak for a while. So,

I thought, this is it at last. This is the fairy house, and here is the fairy queen sitting at her fairy window.

I told her my name and asked what hers was.

"Marianna," she said.

I got up and went to the window. Looking out, I saw a distant mountain pass. Even farther away I could see a green valley. Now it looked strange to me, even though I had come from there that morning.

"Marianna," I said to her, "you must find this view very pleasant."

"Oh, sir," she said, tears starting in her eyes, "I used to. The first time I looked out of this window I said, 'I will never, *never*, grow weary of this.'"

"And what makes you weary of it now?" I asked.

"I don't know," she said, as a tear fell. "But the trouble is not the view—it is Marianna."

Then she told me a little about herself. Some months back, she and her brother had come here from the other side of the mountains. The two had been orphans for many years. Marianna's brother was only 17, but he worked as a woodcutter to support them. The girl made a little money sewing.

No one had lived in the old house for many years. It was not in very good shape. They did not choose it because they liked it so much. They moved into it because it was near the woods and because it was empty.

Marianna's brother worked long hours, sometimes until after dark. Now and then he would be gone for more than a day. He was always tired. After work, he usually ate his dinner and then went to bed. They never had visitors.

It was a lonely life for them both.

I was standing by the window as she told her story. She noticed that I was looking out to the valley below. "Do you know who lives down there?" she said. "I have never been down there myself."

She walked over to the window and pointed down the mountain to the valley. "See there—where the white shines out? The house is made of white marble. It's the only house in sight."

I looked at it for quite a while before I realized what it was. It was no house of marble. It was my own wooden house. The gleam of my house, as seen from here, was like the gleam of this mountain house, as seen from my piazza! The haze made it appear less like a farmhouse than like Prince Charming's palace.

"I have often wondered who lives there," Marianna said. "It must be some very happy person. I was just thinking about it again this morning."

"Some happy person?" I said. "And why do you think that? Do you think a rich person lives there?"

"Rich or not, I don't know," Marianna said. "But it looks so happy. I can't tell how, and it is so far away. Sometimes I think that house is just a dream. You should see it in a sunset."

"No doubt the sunset makes it seem golden," I said. "But no more than the sunrise makes your house seem golden."

"This house?" she said. "The sun is a good sun, but it could never make this house golden. Why should it? This old house is rotting. That is why it is so mossy. In the morning the sun comes in at this old window, to be sure—but it almost blinds me, it is so bright."

She held up an old apron. "I have to use this as a curtain to shut it out. You think that the sun makes this house golden? Not that I ever saw!"

"But," I said, "that's because when the roof shines most, you are inside sewing."

"And why not?" she said. "That is the hottest, weariest part of the day. Sir, the sun doesn't make this roof golden. The sun scorches the roof and then rots it. My brother had to shingle it because it leaked so much. In the winter this house is not fit for a fox to make a den in. The chimney gets blocked with snow like a hollow tree."

"Yours are such gloomy thoughts, Marianna," I said.

"They just reflect things as they are," she answered.

"Then you think only of gloomy things," I said.

"Maybe so," she said, and started sewing again.

I said nothing, but looked out the window again. A wide shadow floated across the land.

"Are you looking at the cloud?" asked Marianna.

"Not at the cloud," I said. "I am looking at the *shadow* of the cloud. But how could you see that while you were sewing?"

"The room got darker," she said. "But now the cloud is gone. And I see that Tray is coming back."

"Tray?" I said.

"That's what I call the shaggy dog," she said. "In the afternoon, he lies down near the door. Don't you see him?"

"You are looking at your sewing," I said. "What are you talking about?"

"Over there," she said, "by the window."

"Oh," I said. "You mean *that* shadow. It does look like a big shaggy dog. I see just what you mean. When the cloud's shadow covers it, the dog goes away. When the cloud is gone, the dog comes back. But what makes the big dog's shadow?"

"You will have to go outside to see that," Marianna said.

"I guess it's one of those grassy rocks," I said.

"You can see how it makes the dog's face shaggy," Marianna said, without looking up.

"You speak as if *you* saw it," I said. "But your eyes never leave your work."

"I know that Tray is looking at you now," she said. "It is the hour when he does that."

"You have been sitting at this window for a long time," I said. "These lifeless shadows are like living friends to you. Even when you don't see them, you know where they are."

"I never thought of it that way," she said. "But if they are friends, the friendliest shadow has been taken from me. It will never return. It was the shadow of a birch tree that used to keep me cool in the hottest part of the day. The tree was struck by lightning and my brother cut it up. You saw the pile of birch sticks outside. The root lies buried there, but the shadow is gone. It will never come back again."

Then another cloud passed overhead, blocking out the shadow of the dog. The air was dead quiet.

"Birds, Marianna, singing birds," I said. "I hear none. I hear nothing. I hear no sounds of children. Don't children ever come around to pick berries?"

"I seldom hear birds," Marianna said. "And children never come around here. This is not the best place for berries."

"But yellow birds showed me the way," I said.

"And then they flew back," she said. "I guess they play about the mountainside. But they don't make their nests at the top. The only sounds here are the sounds of thunder and trees falling."

She kept sewing as she spoke. "No doubt you think my life here is very lonesome," she went on. "You must think that's why I talk of gloomy things, as you call them. Well, I wish I could work in the open air like my brother. Maybe it would tire me enough to take my mind off my loneliness. But I am stuck here, sitting all day at my work."

"But do you not ever go for walks sometimes?" I asked. "These woods are very wide."

"And they are lonesome," she said, "because they are so wide. Sometimes I go a little way into the woods, but I come back soon. At least I *know* the shadows around the house. The ones in the woods are strangers."

"But at night you must get some relief," I said.

"No," Marianna said. "It's just like the day. Thinking, thinking—it's a wheel that I can't stop from turning. It keeps me from getting a good night's sleep."

"Some say that it is helpful to say prayers, then lay your head on a pillow stuffed with herbs—"

"Look!" Marianna said. Through the window she pointed down the hill to a small garden. I could see a patch of herbs. "I've tried an herb pillow," she said. "It didn't help."

"And you have tried prayer?" I asked.

"Both prayer and pillow," she said.

"Is there no other cure or charm?" I asked.

"Oh," she said pointing out the window, "if I could only once get to that house! If I could just see the happy person who lives there! But it's a foolish thought. I don't know why I think it. Maybe it is because I am so lonesome and know nothing."

"I, too, know nothing," I said. "I can't give you the answer to your problem. But I wish I were the happy person in the happy house you dream about. Then, when you looked at me, your sadness might leave you."

Soon I said good-by and headed for my home.

I have not tried to find fairyland again. I still go out on my piazza to sit and look. It is like being in a theater. The scenery is magical—just like a dream. Sometimes in the day I can see the golden light shining on the fairy window. How far from me is the sad face behind it!

But when night comes, truth comes in with the darkness. No light shines from the mountain. I walk back and forth on my piazza, haunted by Marianna's face and her sad story.

The Fiddler

What makes a person a
genius? Do genius and fame
always go together? In this
story a talented young poet
yearns for recognition.
Nothing will make him
happy until he gets it. But
then he meets another
talented man with a very
different point of view. Does
the fiddler know something
that the poet doesn't?

"As I listened, my dark mood got brighter. I was caught by the magic of his fiddle playing."

The Fiddler

So they say my poem is no good! Lasting fame is not for me! I am nobody forever and ever!

Snatching my hat, I threw away the newspaper, and rushed out into Broadway. There, a noisy crowd was headed to a circus in a side street nearby. It had just opened and was well known for the clown who was starring in it.

Just then my old friend Standard came up to me.

"Hello, Helmstone, my boy!" he said. "Ah! What is the matter? You haven't been committing murder? Not running from the police, are you? You look wild!"

"You have seen it, then?" said I. Of course I was talking about the newspaper's review of my poem.

"Oh, yes," Standard said, "I was there at the morning performance. Great clown, I promise you. But here comes my friend Hautboy!"

I didn't have the time—nor did I wish to resent—Standard's mistake. I shook his friend's hand and introduced myself. In a strange way, I was soothed as soon as I looked at his face. He was short and full-bodied, with a youthful, lively look. His face was a bit red and his eyes were honest and cheery. Only the gray in his hair betrayed that he was not just an overgrown boy. From his hair, I guessed he was about 40 or so.

"Come, Standard," Hautboy said to his friend, "are you not coming to the circus? The clown is wonderful, they

say. And you come, too, Mr. Helmstone,"
he said. "After the circus we'll all go to
a restaurant for dinner."

The good humor and sincere looks of
Hautboy acted upon me like magic. It
seemed natural to accept the invitation
of a man with such a kind heart.

During the circus performance, I kept
my eye more on Hautboy than on the
famous clown. Hautboy was the sight for
me. His enjoyment showed what real
happiness could be. He seemed to think
the clown's jokes were wonderful. He
laughed, he stamped his feet, he clapped
his hands. He kept turning to Standard
and me to see if we shared his pleasure.
In this man of 40, I saw a boy of 12. And
I did not respect him any the less for it.
His joy was honest and natural. He
seemed like one of the old Greek gods
who would be youthful forever.

But as much as I admired Hautboy's
attitude, I was not as happy as he. I kept

thinking about the review of my poem, which kept putting me in a bad mood.

But as I looked around me, my mood changed. The people watching the circus all seemed so happy. When the clown did a trick, they laughed and clapped their hands.

Then I thought again of my poem. Who cared if the newspaper man didn't like it? I thought it was one of my best. What if I jumped into the ring with the clown and began to read my poem out loud? Would the crowd cheer for me? Would they clap their hands and stamp their feet? Would they applaud a poet as they applauded a clown?

No! They would hoot at me and call me crazy.

Yet what does that prove? Does it mean I think too much of my poem? Or does it just mean the people don't understand how good it is? Perhaps both are true— the first, for sure.

But why complain? Who wants praise from people more interested in clowns than in poets? What do they know?

I looked at the crowd in the stands, and my eyes landed on Hautboy again. He was laughing at another of the clown's tricks. It was an innocent, honest laugh. He did not know how it hurt my feelings.

When the circus was over we went to a restaurant. Among crowds of others we sat down at one of the tables. Hautboy sat across from me. He was no longer laughing the way he had been at the circus. But he still had a happy look on his face.

He and Standard did most of the talking. I had little to say. But I paid attention to what they were talking about. I was more and more struck by what Hautboy had to say. He seemed to show good sense in everything. He seemed to base all his ideas on facts and reason.

After a while he stood up from the table. He said he was sorry, but he had to meet someone. We all said good-by, and he left.

"Well, Helmstone," said Standard, drumming his fingers on the table, "what do you think of Hautboy?"

"I owe you a thousand thanks for introducing us," I said. "He's certainly an outstanding fellow."

"You like him, then?" said Standard.

"I like and admire him very much," I said. "I wish *I* were Hautboy."

"Ah? That's a pity, now," Standard said. "There's only one Hautboy in the world."

That set me to thinking, and it brought back my dark mood.

"He's very cheerful," I said, "but I guess he was born that way. It's nothing that he has had to work at. It comes to him naturally. His great good sense is plain to see. But a man can have great good sense without being a genius. In fact,

Hautboy should feel lucky that he is *not* a genius."

"You don't think he's a genius?" Standard said.

"Genius?" I said. "What, such a fat, jolly fellow a genius? You'll find that geniuses are thin and not cheerful."

"Maybe he *used to be* a genius," Standard said. "But, maybe he gave up being a genius and became fat instead."

"It's impossible for a person to give up being a genius," I said.

"Ah! You seem very sure of that," Standard said.

"Yes, Standard," I cried. "Your cheery Hautboy is no model for you or me to follow. He has only average ability. His ideas are clear because they are simple. He is cheerful because that's the way he was born. You and I are above that. We are thinkers! We are dreamers!

"Hautboy has never put himself in a position where he could be applauded—

or not. He has never been attacked by people who don't understand him. If he had been, you would see a different Hautboy! He doesn't take the chances that I take. He just slides through life."

"Ah," Standard said.

"Why do you keep saying '*Ah*' to me that way whenever I speak?" I grumbled.

"Did you ever hear of Master Betty?" Standard said.

"Yes," I replied. "He was an English genius who became famous in London."

"The same," said Standard, drumming his fingers on the table.

I looked at him for a moment. What was he getting at? Did this Master Betty have something to do with what we were talking about?

"Master Betty was a 12-year-old English genius," I said. "Hautboy is a normal, 40-year-old American. What in heaven could Master Betty have to do with Hautboy?"

"Oh, nothing in the least," Standard said. "I don't imagine that they ever saw each other. Besides, Master Betty must be dead and buried by now."

"Then why dig him up?" I said. "We are talking about a living person."

"I guess I'm just absent-minded," Standard said. "I beg your pardon. Let's just talk about Hautboy. You think he never had genius. You think he's too fat and happy for that, right? You don't think we can learn a lesson from him? You admire his cheerfulness, but you think it makes him too ordinary? Poor Hautboy—how sad that his cheerfulness should make people think less of him."

"I don't say I think *less* of him," I said. "You are not being fair. I just said that he is no model for me to follow."

Then a sudden noise at my side caught my ear. Turning, I saw that Hautboy had come back. He sat down in the chair he had left a little earlier.

"I finished my business sooner than I expected," Hautboy said. "I thought I'd come back and join you. But come! You have sat here long enough. Let's go to my place. It is only a five-minute walk from here."

"If you will promise to fiddle for us, we will," said Standard.

My mouth dropped open in surprise. Fiddle! Hautboy is a *fiddler*? No wonder there is no trace of genius in the man! By now my mood was darker than ever.

"I will gladly fiddle for you," said Hautboy to Standard. "Come with me."

In a few minutes we found ourselves at Hautboy's place. It was on the fifth floor of an old building. His rooms were cozy, clean and comfortable.

Soon after we got there, Hautboy took out his dented old fiddle. He sat down on an old stool. Then he began to play "Yankee Doodle" and some other old-fashioned songs. But as common as the tunes were, I was caught by their magic. There was something very special about the way Hautboy played them. He looked very ordinary as he sat there on the old stool, wearing his hat tipped to the side of his head. There was nothing special about the way he tapped his foot as he played. But as I listened, my dark mood got brighter. I was caught by the magic of his fiddle playing.

"Pretty good, isn't it?" Standard said. He smiled and winked at me.

"His playing has charmed me," I said.

At last Hautboy stopped playing and put his fiddle down. I looked at him to see if I could see a touch of genius. But he looked just as ordinary as ever. I couldn't figure him out.

After Standard and I left him, we stopped in the street to talk. I begged Standard to tell me more about Hautboy.

"Why, you saw him yourself," Standard said. "And didn't you tell me all about him after he left the restaurant? You told me that there could be no genius in such a fat, cheerful man. I'm sure your own great wisdom has already told you all you need to know about Hautboy."

"Stop making fun of me!" I said. "There is some mystery about Hautboy. Please tell me who the man really is."

"He's a great genius," Standard said. "When he was young, he was very famous. He went from city to city playing his fiddle. The wisest people thought he was just wonderful. Beautiful women admired him. He got praise from the thousands and thousands of people who came to hear him play. But today he walks along Broadway and nobody knows him. Once he wore the crown of success. Now he just wears his old hat. Once he became rich by playing his fiddle before huge crowds. Now he makes his living by teaching others how to play the fiddle. He used to be a famous genius.

Now he is a genius *without* fame. And he is as happy as he can be."

"Tell me what his real name is," I said to Standard.

"Let me whisper it into your ear," Standard said. He leaned toward me and told me a name that had once been famous around the world.

"What?" I cried out. "Oh, Standard! As a child I once heard him play in the theater. I have never forgotten it. The audience went wild applauding him."

Then Standard suddenly changed the subject. "I have heard that your latest poem was not very well received. It got a bad review in the paper."

"Forget it!" I cried out. "Why should I worry about a thing like fame? What does fame matter if a genius like Hautboy can live happily without it?"

Next day I tore up all my poems. I bought myself a fiddle, and now I take regular lessons from Hautboy.

The Lightning-Rod Man

Has fear ever made you do
something you didn't want
to do? This is the story of a
fast-talking salesman. Why
does he only make calls
during a thunderstorm?
Will Mother Nature help
him get an order?

"IN NATURE, THERE IS NO PROTECTION FROM LIGHTNING. BUT I CAN MAKE YOUR HOUSE SAFE WITH A FEW WAVES OF THIS WAND."

The Lightning-Rod Man

What great thunder! thought I, as I looked out the window of my mountain home. The bolts boomed overhead and crashed down on the valley below. Every bolt was followed by a lightning flash. I could hear the rain hitting hard against my roof.

I have always liked thunder. And to me it sounds more glorious on a mountain *more loud* than in the valley.

Then I heard knocking. Someone was at my door. Who was this that chooses a time of thunder for making a call? And why doesn't he use the door knocker?

But what difference did that make? I opened the door.

"Good day, sir," the man said, as I let him in. He was a stranger, and he carried an odd-looking walking stick.

"Pray be seated," I said to him. "It's a fine thunderstorm, sir."

"Fine?" he said. "It's awful!"

"You are wet," I said. "Come stand over here by the fire."

"No," he said, "not for the world!"

The stranger stayed in the exact middle of the room. I took a closer look at him. He was a lean, gloomy figure with long dark hair and deep-set eyes. The whole man was dripping. He stood in a puddle on the bare wood floor.

The man's walking stick was a wooden staff about five feet long. It had two strange-looking balls of green glass at the top. Attached to the glass balls was a copper rod that ended in a three-pointed fork. It looked something like a pitchfork. He held it by the wooden shaft.

"Sir," I said, bowing politely, "have I the honor of a visit from the great Greek god Jupiter? I've seen pictures of him with a lightning bolt in his hands. It looked something like your walking stick. If you are he, I must thank you for this wonderful storm. It is an honor to have you visit my house."

I moved a chair near to the fire. "Here," I said, "this chair is not so nice as your throne, but it is comfortable. Please take a seat and get warm."

The stranger paid no attention to the chair. But he eyed me half in wonder and half in horror.

"Please take a seat," I said again. "You should dry off before you leave here."

Still he paid no attention to the chair. He stayed in the middle of the room. "Excuse me, sir," said he, when at last he spoke. "Instead of accepting your invitation, I think *you* should accept *mine*. I warn you, you had better join me in the middle of the room."

Just then a roar of thunder sounded. "Good heavens!" he cried. "There is another of those awful crashes. I warn you, sir—get away from the fireplace!"

"Mr. Jupiter," I said, "I am happy standing right where I am."

"Are you that ignorant?" he said. "The fireplace is the most dangerous place to stand in such a terrible storm."

"I didn't know that," I said, stepping toward the middle of the room.

The stranger made such an angry face that I couldn't help stepping back toward the fireplace.

"For heaven's sake," he cried, "get *away* from there! Don't you know that the heated air and the soot attract the lightning? To say nothing of the ironwork in the fireplace! Get away from there—I command you!"

"Mr. Jupiter," I said, "I am not used to being commanded in my own house."

"Don't call me by that name," he said. "You are not being serious in a time of terror."

"Sir, will you be so good as to tell me what your business is?" I said. "If you want shelter from the storm, you are welcome. But if you are here on business, tell me so. Who are you, and what do you want?"

"I am a dealer in lightning rods," said the stranger in a softer voice. "My special business is—"

Just then the thunder clapped again. "Good heavens! What a crash!" he said. Then he continued. "Have you ever been struck—your house, I mean—by lightning?"

He banged his walking stick on the floor. "In nature," he said, "there is no protection from lightning. But I can make your house safe with a few waves of this wand." He held the strange walking stick high to give me a better view of it.

"Tell me more," I said.

"My special business," he said, "is to travel around the countryside selling lightning rods. This is one of them." He tapped his staff on the floor again. "I have many happy customers. Last month in the town of Criggan, I put up 23 rods on only five buildings."

"Let me think," I said. "Wasn't it in Criggan that the church steeple and the big elm tree were hit by lightning? Didn't that happen right around midnight last Saturday night? Were any of your rods there?"

"Not on the tree, but on the steeple," he said.

"Then of what use are your lightning rods?" I asked.

"Of life-and-death use," he said. "The workman at the church made a mistake. He let the rod touch part of the tin roof.

That caused the accident. It wasn't my fault, but his."

Thunder crashed again. "Listen!" he cried out.

"I heard it," I said. "But tell me, did you hear about what happened in Montreal last year? A girl was hit by lighting because she was holding metal beads. Do you sell lightning rods in Canada?"

"No," he said. "I think they use only iron rods there. They should use mine, which are of copper. They are much better than iron. The iron rods are too thin. There is not enough body in them to conduct the full electric current. The metal melts and then the building is destroyed. My copper rods never act like that. The people in Canada are fools. *Mine* is the only true rod. Look at it. Only one dollar a foot."

The thunder clapped louder than ever. Now the stranger put his right hand on his left wrist. He began taking his pulse. It was his way of measuring the time between thunder bolts.

"Crash!" he cried. "Only three pulses. It's less than a third of a mile off. I think it's over that oak forest now. I passed it on the way here. Did you know that oak draws more lightning than other trees? It has more iron in its sap."

He looked down at the floor. "This seems to be of oak."

"It is," I said. "I suppose you like to go out in stormy weather, don't you? It must be the best time to try to sell your lighning rods."

"Listen!" he said again, "it's awful!"

I shook my head. "For someone who would protect others from fear, you seem very afraid yourself. Most people choose fair weather for travel. You choose storms, and yet—"

"True, I travel in storms," he said. "But I'm a lightning-rod man, and I know how to be careful. Look at this rod. It's only one dollar a foot."

"A very fine rod, I'm sure," I said. "Now tell me the specific ways you are careful. But, first, let me close the shutters and put a bar across the window."

"Are you mad?" he said. "Don't touch that iron bar! Don't you know that iron attracts lightning?"

"I will just close the shutters, then," I said. "Let me ring for my servant. He will bring me a wooden bar."

"Are you crazy?" the stranger said. "That bell wire might blast you. *Never* touch a bell wire in a storm."

"Is there any way to be safe?" I asked. "Is there any part of the house that I can touch?"

"There is," he said, "but not where you're standing now. Come away from the wall. Sometimes the current will run down a wall. Since a man is a better conductor than a wall, the lighting will leave the wall and run into him. Oh! *That* one must be very close."

"Tell me," I said, "what is the safest spot in the house?"

"This room," he said, "and right where I am standing. Come here."

"Tell me the reasons first," I said.

"Oh! There's another bolt," he said. "Come quickly!"

"Thank you," I said, "but I'll stay where I am. And now, Mr. Lightning-Rod Man, please tell me something. Why is this the safest room? And why is the middle of the room the safest spot in it?"

"This is a one-story house," he said. "You have an attic and a cellar—and this room is between them. Think about it. Lightning sometimes passes from the clouds to the earth. And sometimes it passes from the earth to the clouds. Do you understand? If lighting did strike the house, it would come down the chimney or the walls. That's why the middle of the room is the safest. Now, please—over here!"

"In a moment," I said. "But something you said has made me less afraid."

"What was that?" he said.

"You said that lightning sometimes passes from the earth to the clouds," I said.

"The returning stroke," he said. "When the earth is already full of electricity, it flashes the overflow upwards."

"I see," I said. "Now why don't you come over to the fireplace and get dry?"

"I am better off here, and better off wet," he said.

"Why is that?"

"Getting very wet is the safest thing that you can do in a thunderstorm. Wet clothes are better conductors than the body is. If the lightning strikes, it might pass down the wet clothes without touching the body."

The thunder shook the sky once more.

"Have you got a rug?" the lightning-rod man asked. "Rugs are non-conductors. Get one for me, and one for you, too."

I got one for him, as the thunder grew louder and louder.

"So," I said, "let me hear how you travel safely in a storm."

"Wait till this one is passed," he said.

"No," I said, "tell me about it now. You're standing in the safest place in the house. Go on."

"Briefly, then," he said. "I avoid pine trees, high houses, lonely barns, fields, running water, cows and horses, and crowds of people. If I travel by foot, I do not walk fast. If I am in a buggy, I do not touch its back or sides. If I'm on a horse, I get off and lead the horse. But of all things, I avoid tall men."

"Am I dreaming?" I said. "Man avoids man? And in a time of danger, too?"

"*Of course* I avoid tall men in a thunderstorm! Are you ignorant? Don't you know that a six-foot-tall man will attract lightning? If he stands near running water, it's even worse. The lightning will use him as a conductor to get to the water! Yes, a man is a fine conductor of lightning. The lightning goes through and through him. It only peels a tree."

He thought about it for a moment, and then went on. "You have asked many questions. Now let's get down to our business. Will you order one of my rods? Look at this one."

He held the walking stick up for me to see.

"See," he said. "It is made of the best copper. Copper is the best conductor. Your house is low, but it is on a mountain. Its lowness doesn't help you any. In the mountains, a lightning-rod man does his best business."

He waved the rod. "Look at this," he said. "Just one rod will be enough for a house as small as this. One rod, sir! And a 20-foot rod would only cost 20 dollars."

Another roar of thunder sounded.

"Listen," he said, "that was the loudest yet. It must have struck close by. Anyway, will you order? It's only 20 dollars—a dollar a foot. Shall I put down your name? Think of being burned to ashes in one stroke. All in one flash!"

I laughed. "You pretend to know all about the dangers of nature. In that way, you make people afraid. You say that you can save everyone with your wonderful invention. But what if it breaks or rusts away? Who gave *you* the power to stop nature?

"The days of our lives are numbered. We must all take risks in this world. But in thunder and in sunshine, I am at ease. Away with you! Look now, the storm has passed. The house is unharmed. The God that made the blue sky and the rainbow does not make war against our earth."

"You wretch!" shouted the stranger. His look grew even darker, even as the weather outside grew brighter. There were circles around his eyes like storm clouds. Suddenly he sprang toward me, aiming his forked lightning rod at my heart.

I grabbed it from him. I snapped it, threw it on the floor, and stamped on it. Then I took him by the back of his neck and pushed him out of my house. I threw his broken walking stick out after him.

Later, I told all my neighbors all about him. But I have heard that the lightning-rod man still travels about in storm time. And he still does a good business by playing on people's fears.

What made him not fear

Thinking About
the Stories

The Piazza

1. All the events in a story are arranged in a certain order, or sequence. Tell about one event from the beginning of this story, one from the middle, and one from the end. How are these events related?

2. The plot is the series of events that takes place in a story. Usually, story events are linked in some way. Can you name an event in this story that was the cause of a later event?

3. All stories fit into one or more categories. Is this story serious or funny? Would you call it an adventure, a love story, or a mystery? Is it a character study? Or is it simply a picture the author has painted of a certain time and place? Explain your thinking.

The Fiddler

1. Which character in this story do you most admire? Why? Which character do you like the least?

2. What is the title of this story? Can you think of another good title?

3. Interesting story plots often have unexpected twists and turns. What surprises did you find in this story?

The Lightning-Rod Man

1. Who is the main character in this story? Who are one or two of the minor characters? Describe each of these characters in one or two sentences.

2. Look back at the illustration that introduces this story. What character or characters are pictured? What is happening in the scene? What clues does the picture give you about the time and place of the story?

3. How important is the background of the story? Is weather a factor in the story? Is there a war going on or some other unusual circumstance? What influence does the background have on the characters' lives?

Thinking About
the Book

1. Choose your favorite illustration in this book. Use this picture as a springboard to write a new story. Give the characters different names. Begin your story with something they are saying or thinking.

2. Compare the stories in this book. Which was the most interesting? Why? In what ways were they alike? In what ways different?

3. Good writers usually write about what they know best. If you wrote a story, what kind of characters would you create? What would be the setting?